What Color Is Your Parachute

What Color Is Your Parachute

WORKBOOK

How to Create a Picture of Your Ideal Job or Next Career

by Richard N. Bolles

TEN SPEED PRESS
Berkeley | Toronto

The Flower Exercise

A PICTURE OF THE JOB OF YOUR DREAMS

In order to hunt for your ideal job, or even something close to your ideal job, you must have a picture of it, in your head. The clearer the picture, the easier it will be to hunt for it. The purpose of this exercise is to guide you as you draw that picture.

We have chosen a "Flower" as the model for that picture. While such expressions as "plugging in," "turning on," and other common phrases portray you (implicitly) as a machine, you are actually much more like a Flower than a machine. That is to say, you flourish in some job environments, but wither in others. Therefore, the purpose of putting together this Flower Picture of yourself is to help you identify what kind of a work climate you will flourish in, and thus do your very best work. Your twin goals should be to be as happy as you can be at your job, while at the same time you do your most effective work.

There is a picture of the Flower on pages 6 and 7 that you can use as your worksheet.

As you can see, skills are at the center of the Flower, even as they are at the center of your mission, career, or job. They are listed in order of priority.

Surrounding them are six petals. Listed in the order in which you will work on them, they are:

1. Geography
2. Interests (Fields of Fascination)
3. People Environments
4. Values
5. Working Conditions
6. Salary & Level of Responsibility

When you are done filling in these skills and petals, you will have the complete Flower picture of your Ideal Job. Okay? Then, get out your pen or pencil and let's get started.

The Flower

A Picture of the Job of Your Dreams

5
WITH
**MY FAVORITE
WORKING
CONDITIONS:**

1.

2.

3.

4.

5.

My fourth:

My fifth:

My sixth:

3
IN ORGANIZATIONS
HAVING
**MY FAVORITE
PEOPLE
ENVIRONMENTS:**

1.

2.

3.

4.

5.

6.

R   I

C   A

E   S

4
SERVING
MY FAVORITE VALUES:

1.

2.

3.

4.

5.

6.

Example (Six Favorite Skills)

My Favorite
Skill is:

Writing

My Second
Favorite Skill is:

Crafting

My Third:

*Precision-
working*

My Fourth:

*Planning
and
Directing*

My Fifth:

Inventing

My Sixth:

*Program-
ming*

Your Favorite Transferable Skills

We begin with skills. You must, first of all, identify your favorite transferable skills that you most enjoy using, *in order of priority or importance to you.* Here are the five steps to accomplishing that.

1. Write Your First Story

To do this, you will need to write **seven stories** about things you did just because they were fun, or because they gave you a sense of adventure, or gave you a sense of accomplishment. It does not matter whether anyone else ever knew about this accomplishment, or not. Each story can be about something you did at work, or in school, or at play—and can be from any time period of your life. It should not be more than two or three paragraphs in length.

Below is a form to help you write each of your Seven Stories. (You will obviously want to go down to Kinko's or your local copy shop and make seven copies of this form before you begin filling it out for the first time. The copies work best if you make them on seven pieces of 8½″ x 11″ paper.)

After you have written your first story, we will show you how to analyze it for the transferable skills that you used therein.

MY SEVEN LIFE STORIES

Column 1	Column 2	Column 3	Column 4	Column 5
Your Goal: What You Want to Accomplish	Some Kind of Obstacle (or limit, hurdle, or restraint you had to overcome before it could be accomplished)	What You Did Step-by-Step (It may help if you pretend you are telling this story to a whining 4-year-old child who keeps asking, after each of your sentences, "An' then whadja do? An' then whadja do?")	Description of the Result (What you accomplished)	Any Measure or Quantities to Prove Your Achievement

2. Analyze the Story for Transferable Skills

Once you have written Story #1 (and before you write the other six), you will want to analyze it for the transferable skills you *used*. (You can decide later if you loved those skills or not. For now, just do an inventory.)

To do this inventory, go to the list of Skills Keys found on pages 11 to 13, which resemble a series of typewriter keys. Transferable skills divide into:

1. Physical Skills: the transferable skills you enjoy, using primarily *your hands or body*—with things, or nature;

2. Mental Skills: the transferable skills you enjoy, using primarily *your mind*—with data/information, ideas, or subjects;

3. Interpersonal Skills: the transferable skills you enjoy, involving primarily *personal relationships*—as you serve or help people or animals, and their needs or problems.[1]

Therefore you will find three sets of Skills Keys, labeled accordingly.

As you look at each key in the three sets, the question you need to ask yourself is: "Did I use this transferable skill *in this Story* (#1)?"

That is the *only* question you ask yourself (at the moment). Then you go to the little box named #1 (under each Skill Key), and this is what you do:

Taking
Instructions,
Serving,
or Helping

Did I Use This Skill in Story

Yes [✔] [2] [3] [4] [5] [6] [7]

If the answer is "Yes," fill in the little box, as shown (left).

Ignore the other little boxes for the time being; they belong to your other stories (all the little boxes named #2 belong to Story #2, all the little boxes named #3 belong to Story #3, etc.).

If the answer is "No," leave the box labeled #1 blank, as shown (right).

Taking
Instructions,
Serving,
or Helping

Did I Use This Skill in Story

No [✔] [2] [3] [4] [5] [6] [7]

3. Write Six Other Stories, and Analyze Them for Transferable Skills

Voila! You are done with Story #1. However, "one swallow doth not a summer make," so the fact that you used certain skills in this first Story doesn't tell you much. You are looking for **patterns**—transferable skills that keep reappearing in story after story. They keep reappearing because they are your favorites (assuming you chose stories where you were *really* enjoying yourself).

So, now, write Story #2, from any period in your life, analyze it using the keys, etc., etc. And keep this process up, until you have written, and analyzed, seven stories.

4. Decide Which Skills Are Your Favorites, and Prioritize Them

When you're done writing and analyzing all Seven Stories, you should now go back and look over the three pages of "Skills Keys" to see which skills got used the most often. Make a list.

Cross out any that you don't enjoy using.

Prioritize the remainder, using one of the Prioritizing Grids on pages 15 and 16.

My Physical Skills

I am good at

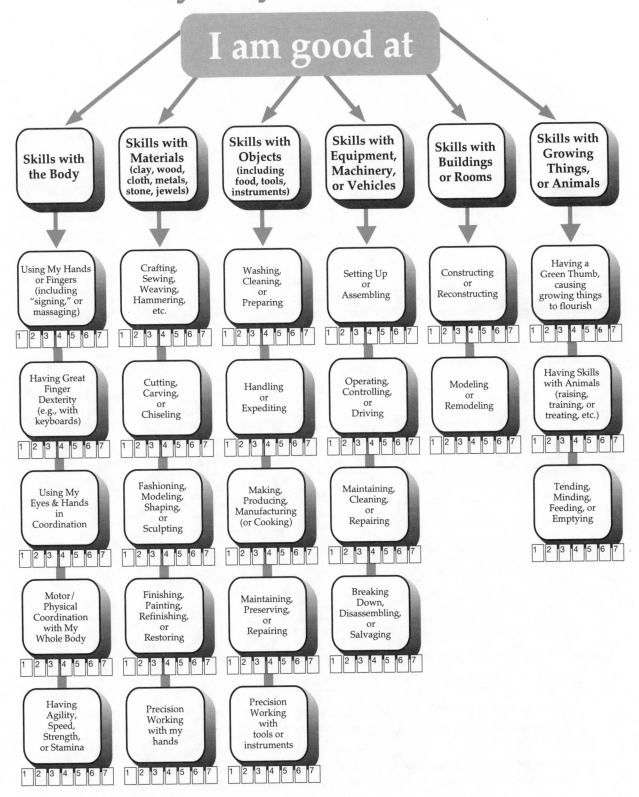

Skills with the Body	Skills with Materials (clay, wood, cloth, metals, stone, jewels)	Skills with Objects (including food, tools, instruments)	Skills with Equipment, Machinery, or Vehicles	Skills with Buildings or Rooms	Skills with Growing Things, or Animals
Using My Hands or Fingers (including "signing," or massaging)	Crafting, Sewing, Weaving, Hammering, etc.	Washing, Cleaning, or Preparing	Setting Up or Assembling	Constructing or Reconstructing	Having a Green Thumb, causing growing things to flourish
1 2 3 4 5 6 7	1 2 3 4 5 6 7	1 2 3 4 5 6 7	1 2 3 4 5 6 7	1 2 3 4 5 6 7	1 2 3 4 5 6 7
Having Great Finger Dexterity (e.g., with keyboards)	Cutting, Carving, or Chiseling	Handling or Expediting	Operating, Controlling, or Driving	Modeling or Remodeling	Having Skills with Animals (raising, training, or treating, etc.)
1 2 3 4 5 6 7	1 2 3 4 5 6 7	1 2 3 4 5 6 7	1 2 3 4 5 6 7	1 2 3 4 5 6 7	1 2 3 4 5 6 7
Using My Eyes & Hands in Coordination	Fashioning, Modeling, Shaping, or Sculpting	Making, Producing, Manufacturing (or Cooking)	Maintaining, Cleaning, or Repairing		Tending, Minding, Feeding, or Emptying
1 2 3 4 5 6 7	1 2 3 4 5 6 7	1 2 3 4 5 6 7	1 2 3 4 5 6 7		1 2 3 4 5 6 7
Motor/ Physical Coordination with My Whole Body	Finishing, Painting, Refinishing, or Restoring	Maintaining, Preserving, or Repairing	Breaking Down, Disassembling, or Salvaging		
1 2 3 4 5 6 7	1 2 3 4 5 6 7	1 2 3 4 5 6 7	1 2 3 4 5 6 7		
Having Agility, Speed, Strength, or Stamina	Precision Working with my hands	Precision Working with tools or instruments			
1 2 3 4 5 6 7	1 2 3 4 5 6 7	1 2 3 4 5 6 7			

My Mental Skills

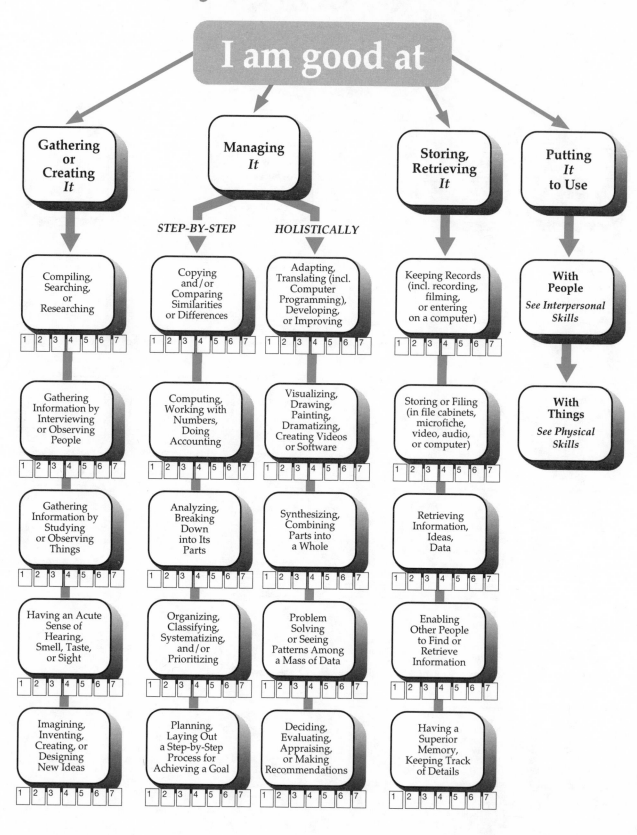

I am good at

Gathering or Creating *It*

Compiling, Searching, or Researching
1 2 3 4 5 6 7

Gathering Information by Interviewing or Observing People
1 2 3 4 5 6 7

Gathering Information by Studying or Observing Things
1 2 3 4 5 6 7

Having an Acute Sense of Hearing, Smell, Taste, or Sight
1 2 3 4 5 6 7

Imagining, Inventing, Creating, or Designing New Ideas
1 2 3 4 5 6 7

Managing *It*

STEP-BY-STEP

Copying and/or Comparing Similarities or Differences
1 2 3 4 5 6 7

Computing, Working with Numbers, Doing Accounting
1 2 3 4 5 6 7

Analyzing, Breaking Down into Its Parts
1 2 3 4 5 6 7

Organizing, Classifying, Systematizing, and/or Prioritizing
1 2 3 4 5 6 7

Planning, Laying Out a Step-by-Step Process for Achieving a Goal
1 2 3 4 5 6 7

HOLISTICALLY

Adapting, Translating (incl. Computer Programming), Developing, or Improving
1 2 3 4 5 6 7

Visualizing, Drawing, Painting, Dramatizing, Creating Videos or Software
1 2 3 4 5 6 7

Synthesizing, Combining Parts into a Whole
1 2 3 4 5 6 7

Problem Solving or Seeing Patterns Among a Mass of Data
1 2 3 4 5 6 7

Deciding, Evaluating, Appraising, or Making Recommendations
1 2 3 4 5 6 7

Storing, Retrieving *It*

Keeping Records (incl. recording, filming, or entering on a computer)
1 2 3 4 5 6 7

Storing or Filing (in file cabinets, microfiche, video, audio, or computer)
1 2 3 4 5 6 7

Retrieving Information, Ideas, Data
1 2 3 4 5 6 7

Enabling Other People to Find or Retrieve Information
1 2 3 4 5 6 7

Having a Superior Memory, Keeping Track of Details
1 2 3 4 5 6 7

Putting *It* to Use

With People
See Interpersonal Skills

With Things
See Physical Skills

My Interpersonal Skills

I am good with

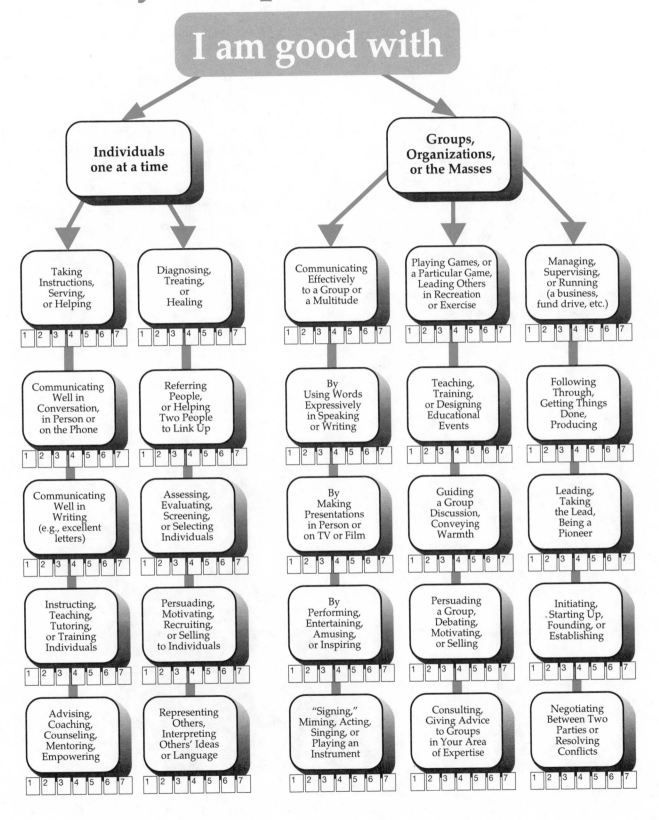

Individuals one at a time

Taking Instructions, Serving, or Helping
1 2 3 4 5 6 7

Communicating Well in Conversation, in Person or on the Phone
1 2 3 4 5 6 7

Communicating Well in Writing (e.g., excellent letters)
1 2 3 4 5 6 7

Instructing, Teaching, Tutoring, or Training Individuals
1 2 3 4 5 6 7

Advising, Coaching, Counseling, Mentoring, Empowering
1 2 3 4 5 6 7

Diagnosing, Treating, or Healing
1 2 3 4 5 6 7

Referring People, or Helping Two People to Link Up
1 2 3 4 5 6 7

Assessing, Evaluating, Screening, or Selecting Individuals
1 2 3 4 5 6 7

Persuading, Motivating, Recruiting, or Selling to Individuals
1 2 3 4 5 6 7

Representing Others, Interpreting Others' Ideas or Language
1 2 3 4 5 6 7

Groups, Organizations, or the Masses

Communicating Effectively to a Group or a Multitude
1 2 3 4 5 6 7

By Using Words Expressively in Speaking or Writing
1 2 3 4 5 6 7

By Making Presentations in Person or on TV or Film
1 2 3 4 5 6 7

By Performing, Entertaining, Amusing, or Inspiring
1 2 3 4 5 6 7

"Signing," Miming, Acting, Singing, or Playing an Instrument
1 2 3 4 5 6 7

Playing Games, or a Particular Game, Leading Others in Recreation or Exercise
1 2 3 4 5 6 7

Teaching, Training, or Designing Educational Events
1 2 3 4 5 6 7

Guiding a Group Discussion, Conveying Warmth
1 2 3 4 5 6 7

Persuading a Group, Debating, Motivating, or Selling
1 2 3 4 5 6 7

Consulting, Giving Advice to Groups in Your Area of Expertise
1 2 3 4 5 6 7

Managing, Supervising, or Running (a business, fund drive, etc.)
1 2 3 4 5 6 7

Following Through, Getting Things Done, Producing
1 2 3 4 5 6 7

Leading, Taking the Lead, Being a Pioneer
1 2 3 4 5 6 7

Initiating, Starting Up, Founding, or Establishing
1 2 3 4 5 6 7

Negotiating Between Two Parties or Resolving Conflicts
1 2 3 4 5 6 7

The Prioritizing Grid

How to Prioritize Your Lists of Anything

Here is a method for taking (say) ten items, and figuring out which one is most important to you, which is next most important, etc.

• Insert the items to be prioritized, in any order, in Section A. Then compare two items at a time, circling the one you prefer—between the two—in Section B. Which one is more important to you? State the question any way you want to: In the case of geographical factors, you might ask, "If I were being offered two jobs, one in an area that had factor #1, but not factor #2; the other in an area that had factor #2, but not factor #1, all other things being equal, which job would I take?" Circle it. Then go on to the next pair, etc.

• When you are all done, count up the number of times each number got circled, all told. Enter these totals on the TIMES line in Section C. Then notice the number of times each item was circled ("Times" = "Times Circled"). This determines the item's ranking. Most circled = #1, next most circled = #2, etc. Enter this ranking on the RANK line in Section C. If two items are circled the same number of times, look back in Section B to see—when those two were compared there—which one you preferred. Give that one an extra half point. List the items, now in their proper rank, in Section D.

> *Since you will be using this Prioritizing Grid more than once in these exercises you will want to go down to Kinko's or your local copy shop and make a number of copies of this form* before *you begin filling it in for the first time.*

The question to ask yourself, on the Grid, as you confront each "pair" is: "If I were offered two jobs, and in one job I could use the first skill, but not the second; while in the other job, I could use the second skill, but not the first, which job would I choose?" When you've got your ten favorite transferable skills, in order, copy the top six onto the Flower Diagram on pages 6 and 7.

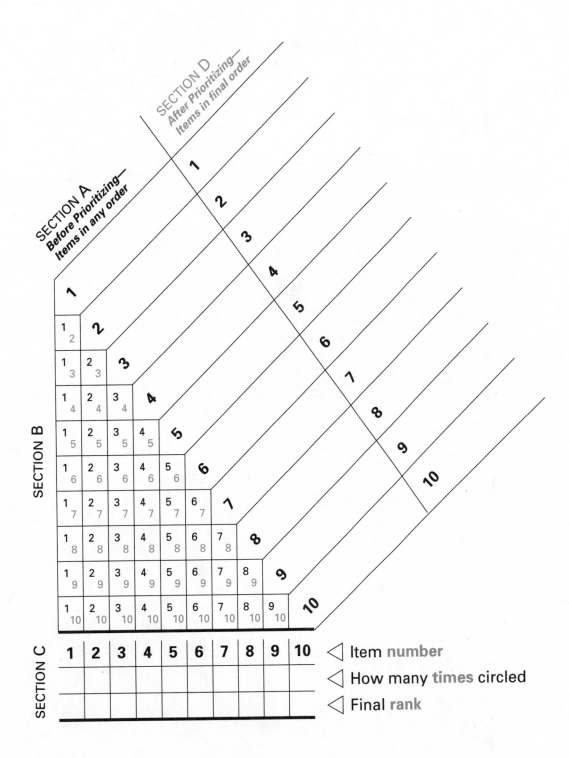

SECTION A
Before Prioritizing—
Items in any order

SECTION D—
After Prioritizing—
Items in final order

SECTION B

SECTION C

◁ Item **number**

◁ How many **times** circled

◁ Final **rank**

Prioritizing Grid
for 10 Items

```
1  1  1  1  1  1  1  1  1  1  1  1  1  1  1  1  1  1  1  1  1  1  1
  2  3  4  5  6  7  8  9  10 11 12 13 14 15 16 17 18 19 20 21 22 23 24

2  2  2  2  2  2  2  2  2  2  2  2  2  2  2  2  2  2  2  2  2  2
  3  4  5  6  7  8  9  10 11 12 13 14 15 16 17 18 19 20 21 22 23 24

3  3  3  3  3  3  3  3  3  3  3  3  3  3  3  3  3  3  3  3  3
  4  5  6  7  8  9  10 11 12 13 14 15 16 17 18 19 20 21 22 23 24

4  4  4  4  4  4  4  4  4  4  4  4  4  4  4  4  4  4  4  4
  5  6  7  8  9  10 11 12 13 14 15 16 17 18 19 20 21 22 23 24

5  5  5  5  5  5  5  5  5  5  5  5  5  5  5  5  5  5  5
  6  7  8  9  10 11 12 13 14 15 16 17 18 19 20 21 22 23 24

6  6  6  6  6  6  6  6  6  6  6  6  6  6  6  6  6  6
  7  8  9  10 11 12 13 14 15 16 17 18 19 20 21 22 23 24

7  7  7  7  7  7  7  7  7  7  7  7  7  7  7  7  7
  8  9  10 11 12 13 14 15 16 17 18 19 20 21 22 23 24

8  8  8  8  8  8  8  8  8  8  8  8  8  8  8  8
  9  10 11 12 13 14 15 16 17 18 19 20 21 22 23 24

9  9  9  9  9  9  9  9  9  9  9  9  9  9  9
  10 11 12 13 14 15 16 17 18 19 20 21 22 23 24

10 10 10 10 10 10 10 10 10 10 10 10 10 10
  11 12 13 14 15 16 17 18 19 20 21 22 23 24

11 11 11 11 11 11 11 11 11 11 11 11 11
  12 13 14 15 16 17 18 19 20 21 22 23 24

12 12 12 12 12 12 12 12 12 12 12 12
  13 14 15 16 17 18 19 20 21 22 23 24

13 13 13 13 13 13 13 13 13 13 13
  14 15 16 17 18 19 20 21 22 23 24

14 14 14 14 14 14 14 14 14 14
  15 16 17 18 19 20 21 22 23 24

15 15 15 15 15 15 15 15 15
  16 17 18 19 20 21 22 23 24

16 16 16 16 16 16 16 16
  17 18 19 20 21 22 23 24

17 17 17 17 17 17 17
  18 19 20 21 22 23 24

18 18 18 18 18 18
  19 20 21 22 23 24

19 19 19 19 19
  20 21 22 23 24

20 20 20 20
  21 22 23 24

21 21 21
  22 23 24

22 22
  23 24

23
  24
```

Total times each number got circled.

1	2	3	4	5	6
7	8	9	10	11	12
13	14	15	16	17	18
19	20	21	22	23	24

Prioritizing Grid for 24 Items

5. "Flesh Out" Your Favorite Transferable Skills with Your Traits

In general, traits describe:

How you deal with time, and promptness.

How you deal with people and emotions.

How you deal with authority, and being told what to do at your job.

How you deal with supervision, and being told how to do your job.

How you deal with impulse vs. self-discipline, within yourself.

How you deal with initiative vs. response, within yourself.

How you deal with crises or problems.

A CHECKLIST
OF MY STRONGEST TRAITS

I am very . . .

❏ Accurate	❏ Discreet	❏ Persevering
❏ Achievement-oriented	❏ Driving	❏ Persistent
❏ Adaptable	❏ Dynamic	❏ Pioneering
❏ Adept	❏ Extremely economical	❏ Practical
❏ Adept at having fun	❏ Effective	❏ Professional
❏ Adventuresome	❏ Energetic	❏ Protective
❏ Alert	❏ Enthusiastic	❏ Punctual
❏ Appreciative	❏ Exceptional	❏ Quick/work quickly
❏ Assertive	❏ Exhaustive	❏ Rational
❏ Astute	❏ Experienced	❏ Realistic
❏ Authoritative	❏ Expert	❏ Reliable
❏ Calm	❏ Firm	❏ Resourceful
❏ Cautious	❏ Flexible	❏ Responsible
❏ Charismatic	❏ Humanly oriented	❏ Responsive
❏ Competent	❏ Impulsive	❏ Safeguarding
❏ Consistent	❏ Independent	❏ Self-motivated
❏ Contagious in my enthusiasm	❏ Innovative	❏ Self-reliant
❏ Cooperative	❏ Knowledgeable	❏ Sensitive
❏ Courageous	❏ Loyal	❏ Sophisticated, very sophisticated
❏ Creative	❏ Methodical	❏ Strong
❏ Decisive	❏ Objective	❏ Supportive
❏ Deliberate	❏ Open-minded	❏ Tactful
❏ Dependable/have dependability	❏ Outgoing	❏ Thorough
❏ Diligent	❏ Outstanding	❏ Unique
❏ Diplomatic	❏ Patient	❏ Unusual
	❏ Penetrating	❏ Versatile
	❏ Perceptive	❏ Vigorous

Once you've checked off your favorites, prioritize them (using another copy of the Prioritizing Grid if necessary), and then integrate your favorites into the building blocks of transferable skills, as described on page 8.

SOME PROBLEMS YOU MAY RUN INTO, WHILE DOING YOUR SKILL-IDENTIFICATION

In trying to identify your skills, it will not be surprising if you run into some problems. Let us look at the five most common ones that have arisen for job-hunters in the past:

1. "When I write my skill stories, I don't know exactly what is an achievement."

When you're looking for a story/achievement to illustrate one of your skills, you're *not* looking for something that only you have done, in the history of the world. What you're looking for is a lot simpler than that. You're looking for *any* time in your life when you did something that was, at that time of your life, a source of pride and accomplishment *for you*. It might have been learning to ride a bike. It might be achieving your first quota, at work. It might be a particularly significant project that you designed, in midlife. It doesn't matter whether or not it pleased anybody else; it only matters that it pleased you.

I like Bernard Haldane's definition of an achievement. He says it is: something you yourself feel you have done well, that you also enjoyed doing and felt proud of. In other words you are looking for an accomplishment which gave you two pleasures: enjoyment while doing it, and satisfaction from the outcome. That doesn't mean you may not have sweated as you did it, or hated *some parts* of the process, but it does mean that

basically you enjoyed *most of* the process. The pleasure was not simply in the outcome, but along the way as well.

2. "I don't see why I should look for skills I enjoy; it seems to me that employers will only want to know what skills I do well. They will not care whether I enjoy using the skill or not."

Well, sure, it is important for you to find the skills you do well, above all else. But, generally speaking, that is hard for you to evaluate about yourself. *Do I do this well, or not? Compared to whom?* Even aptitude tests can't resolve this dilemma for you. So it's better to take the following circular equation, which experience has shown to be true:

If it is a skill you do well, you will generally enjoy it.

If it is a skill you enjoy, it is generally because you do it well.

With these equations in hand, you will see that—since they are equal anyway—it is much more useful to ask yourself, "Do I enjoy doing it?" instead of hunting for the elusive "Do I do it well?" I repeat: listing the skills you most *enjoy* is—in most cases—just another way of listing the skills you do *best*.

The reason why this idea—of making *enjoyment* the key—causes such feelings of uncomfortableness in so many of us is that we have an old historical tradition in this country which insinuates you shouldn't really enjoy yourself in life. To suffer is virtuous.

Sample: Two girls do babysitting. One hates it. One enjoys it thoroughly. Which is more virtuous in God's sight? According to that old tradition, the one who hates it is more virtuous. Some of us feel this instinctively, even if more logical thought says, Whoa!

We have this subconscious fear that if we are caught enjoying life, punishment looms. Thus, the story of two Scotsmen who met on the street one day: "Isn't this a beautiful day?" said one. "Aye," said the other, "but we'll pay for it."

We feel it is okay to talk about our failures, but not about our successes. To talk about our successes appears to be boasting, and that is manifestly a sin. Or so we think. We shouldn't be enjoying so much about ourselves.

But look at the birds of the air, or watch your pets at play. You will notice one distinctive fact about that part of God's creation: when a bird or a pet does what it is meant to do, by God and nature, it manifests true joy.

Joy is so clearly a part of God's plan for us. God wants us to eat; therefore He made eating enjoyable. God wants us to sleep; therefore He made sleeping enjoyable. God wants us to procreate, love, and make love; therefore He made sex enjoyable, and love even more so.

Likewise, God gives to each of us unique combinations of skills and talents which He wants us to contribute to His general plan—to the symphony of the world, and the music of the spheres. Therefore, **when we use the talents He most wants each of us to use, He attends it with a feeling of great joy.** Everywhere in God's plan for His creation, joy rewards right action.

Bad employers will not care whether you enjoy a particular task, or not. But good employers will care greatly. They know that unless a would-be employee has **enthusiasm** for his or her work, the quality of that work will always suffer.

3. *"I have no difficulty finding stories to write up, from my life, that I consider to be enjoyable achievements; but once these are written, I have great difficulty in seeing what the skills are—even if I stare at the skills keys in the Exercises for hours. I need somebody else's insight."*

You may want to consider getting two friends or two other members of your family to sit down with you, and do skill identification through the practice of "Trioing," which I invented some twenty years ago to help with this very problem. This practice is fully described in my book *Where Do I Go from Here with My Life?* But to save you the trouble of reading it, here is—in general—how it goes:

a. Each of the three of you quietly writes up some story of an accomplishment in your life that was enjoyable.

b. Each of the three of you quietly analyzes just your own story to see what skills you see there; you jot these down.

c. One of you then volunteers to go first. You read your story aloud. The other two jot down on a piece of paper whatever skills they hear you using. They ask you to pause if they're having trouble keeping up. You finish your story. You read aloud the skills *you* picked out in that story.

d. Then the second person tells you what's on their list: what skills *they* heard you use in your story. You copy them down, below your own list, even if you don't agree with every one of them.

e. Then the third person tells you what's on their list; what skills *they* heard you use in your story. You copy them down, below your own list, even if you don't agree with every one of them.

f. When they're both done, you ask them any questions for further elaboration that you may have. *"What did you mean by this skill? Where did you think you heard me using it?"*

g. Now it is the next person's turn, and you repeat steps "c" through "f" with them. Then it is the third person's turn, and you repeat steps "c" through "f" with them.

h. Now it is time to move on to a second story for each of you, so you begin with steps "a" through "g" all over again, except that each of you writes a new story. And so on, through seven stories.

4. *"I don't like the skill words you offer in the Exercises. Can't I use my own words, the ones I'm familiar with from my past profession?"*

It's okay to invent your own words for your skills, but it is not useful to state your transferable skills in the jargon of your old profession, such as (in the case of ex-clergy), *"I am good at preaching."* If you are going to choose a new career, out there in what people call the secular world, you must not use language that locks you into the past—or suggests that you were good in one profession but in one profession only. Therefore, it is important to take jargon words such as *preaching* and ask yourself what is its larger form? *"Teaching?"* Perhaps. *"Motivating people?"* Perhaps. *"Inspiring people to the depths of their being?"* Perhaps. Only you can say what is true, for you. But in one way or another be sure to get your skills out of any jargon that locks you into your past career.

'. . . and give me good abstract-reasoning ability, interpersonal skills, cultural perspective, linguistic comprehension, and a high sociodynamic potential.'

5. "Once I've listed my favorite transferable skills, I see immediately a job-title that they point to. Is that okay?"

Nope. Once you've finished your skill-identification, steer clear of prematurely putting a job-title on the skills you see. Skills can point to *many* different jobs, which have a multitude of titles. Therefore, don't lock yourself in, prematurely. *"I'm looking for a job where I can use the following skills,"* is fine. But, *"I'm looking for a job where I can be a (job-title)"* is a no-no, at this point in your job-hunt. Always define **WHAT** you want to do with your life and **WHAT** you have to offer to the world in terms of your favorite talents/gifts/skills—not in terms of a job-title. That way, you can stay mobile in the midst of this constantly changing economy, where you never know what's going to happen next.

PEANUTS reprinted by permission of United Feature Syndicate, Inc.

PETAL #1

Geography

Even if you *love* where you are now, or even if you're *stuck* where you are now, you never know when an opportunity may suddenly open up for you, down the road. You want to be ready. Don't wait until then to do this exercise; do it now!

The question you need to answer is: Where would you most like to live and work, if you had a choice (besides where you are now)? In answering this question, it is important—before you come to names—to list the geographical *factors* that are important to you.

To help you do this, fill out the accompanying chart. *(You may copy it onto a larger piece of paper if you wish, before you begin working on it. And, if you are doing this exercise with a partner, make a copy of the chart for them also before you start filling it out, so that each of you may have a "clean" copy of your own.)*

My Geographical Preferences
Decision Making for Just You

Column 1 Names of Places I Have Lived	Column 2 From the Past: Negatives	Column 3 Translating the Negatives into Positives	Column 4 Ranking of My Positives
	Factors I Disliked and Still Dislike About That Place	Factors I Liked and Still Like About That Place	1. 2. 3. 4. 5. 6. 7. 8. 9. 10.

Column 5		Our Geographical Preferences		
Places That Fit These Criteria		*Decision Making for You and a Partner*		
	Column 6 Ranking of His/Her Preferences	Column 7 Combining Our Two Lists (Columns 4 & 6)	Column 8 Places That Fit These Criteria
	a.	a.	
		1.	
	b.	b.	
		2.	
	c.	c.	
		3.	
	d.	d.	
		4.	
	e.	e.	
		5.	
	f.	f.	
		6.	
	g.	g.	
	h.	7.	
		h.	
	i.	8.	
		i.	
	j.	9.	
		j.	
		10.	

1. **List all the places (towns, cities, etc.) where you have ever lived.** These go in Column 1.

2. **List the factors you *disliked* and still dislike about each place.** Naturally, there will be some repetition. In which case, just put an extra check mark in front of any factor you already have written down, when it comes up again. All of these negative factors go in Column 2.

3. **Then take each of those negative factors and translate the negatives into positives.** This will not *necessarily* be the opposite. For example, "rains all the time" does not necessarily translate into "sunny all the time." It might be more like: "sunny at least 200 days a year." *It's your call.* All these positive factors go in Column 3. Feel free to add at the bottom of the column here any positive factors you remember, off the top of your head, about the places in Column 1.

4. **Now, rank your positive factors list (Column 3) in their order of importance, to you.** They will be things like: "has cultural opportunities," "skiing in the winter," "good newspaper," etc. List your top ten positive factors, in exact order, in Column 4.

If you are baffled as to how to prioritize these factors in exact order, use the Prioritizing Grid on page 15. In using that grid, the question to ask yourself as you confront each "pair" is: "If I could live in a place that had this first 'factor,' but not the second; or if I could live in another place that had the second "factor," but not the first, in which place would I choose to live?"

5. **When you are done, show this list of ten prioritized, positive factors to everyone you know, and ask them what cities, towns, or places they know of that have all or most of these factors.** You want to particularly emphasize the top factors, the ones that are the most important to you. If there is only a partial overlap between your factors and the places your friends suggest, be sure the overlap is in the factors you placed first on your list.

6. **From all the names your friends suggest to you, choose the three that look most intriguing to you, in order of your personal preference, based on what you now know.** These go in Column 5. These are the places you will want to find out more about, until you are sure which is your absolute first preference, second, and third.

7. **Now, go back to the Flower Diagram on page 6, and copy Column 5 (or 8) onto the Geography petal.** You may also, if you wish, copy the first three to five Positives, from Column 4 or 7. Voila! You are done with Geography. You now know the place(s) to find out more about, through their Chamber of Commerce, the Internet, a summer visit, etc.

If you are doing this with a partner, you will not use Column 5. Instead, copy *their* Column 4 into your Column 6. Then alternately combine *their* first five factors and *your* first five factors, until you wind up with a list of ten altogether. (First you list their top one, then your top one, then their second preference, then your second preference, etc.) This goes in Column 7. It is *this* list of ten positive factors which you both then show to *everyone* you know, to ask them what cities, towns, or places they know of that have all or most of these factors, *beginning with the top ones.* From all the names those friends suggest to you, you then choose the three places that look the most intriguing to both of you, and rank them in order. These go in Column 8.

Your Favorite Interests, or "Fields of Fascination"

We are talking here about the major element of "Where?" It follows on the heels of "What?" "What transferable skills, that you have, do you most enjoy using?" "Where?" is a matter of "Where would you most like to use your favorite skills?" In other words, we are talking about Fields, and particularly, those Fields that fascinate you.

Now, there are three basic kinds of Fields or Interests that you may have:

1. Fields That Use Your Mental Skills (the "Subjects list")

2. Fields Dealing with People's Problems or Needs (the "People list")

3. Fields Dealing with Things, Tools, or Products (the "Things list")

Let us do some exercises, dealing with each of them in turn:

1. Fields That Use Your Mental Skills

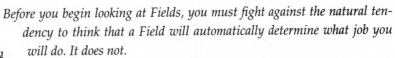

Before you begin looking at Fields, you must fight against the natural tendency to think that a Field will automatically determine what job you will do. It does not.

Think of a Field of Knowledge as, literally, a field—a meadow, a large meadow. Lots of people are standing in that meadow, or Field, no matter what Field it is. And they have many different skills, do many different things, have many different job titles.

Let us take the Field called "Movies" as our example. Suppose you love Movies, and want to choose this Field for your next job or career. Your first instinct will be to think that this automatically means you have to be either an actor or actress, or a screenwriter, or a director, or a movie critic. Not so. There are many other people standing out in that Field, helping to produce Movies. Just look at the closing credits at the end of any movie, and you will see: researchers (especially for movies set in another time), travel experts (to scout locations), interior designers (to design sets), carpenters (to build them), painters (for backdrops, etc.), artists, computer graphics designers (for special effects), costume designers, makeup artists, hairstylists, photographers (camera operators), lighting technicians, sound mixers and sound editors, composers (for sound tracks), conductors, musicians, singers, stunt people, animal trainers, caterers, drivers, first aid people, personal assistants, secretaries, publicists, accountants, etc., etc. My, there are a lot of people standing in that Field—some of whom are outstanding in their Field!

And so it is with any Field. No matter what your skills are, they can be used in any meadow or Field that you may choose as your favorite.

For some people, incidentally, Subjects yield *the least* helpful information about future Fields. Reason? Subjects often *don't* point to jobs. Example? Liberal Arts. But, might as well inventory everything we've learned so far, *just in case* (using the exercise called **The Subjects Chart**). *Then* you can go on to the exercise called **The People List**, and then the exercise called **The Things Phone Book**).

Everyone has mental skills.

Your mental skills are such things as: *the ability to gather information, to analyze information, to organize information, to present information,* and the like. The question here is: **what kinds of information, subjects, bodies of knowledge, ideas, or languages do you like to use your mental skills with?**

In order for you to answer this question, it is helpful to fill out the following chart; *you may first copy it onto a larger piece of paper, if you wish, in order to have more room to write.*

Please note that this chart is asking you what subjects you know *anything* about, whether you *like* the subject or not. (*Later,* you will ask yourself which of these you like or even *love.*) For now, the task facing you is merely *inventory.* That is a task similar to inventorying what clothes you've got in your closet, before you decide which ones to give away. Only, here, *the closet is your head,* and you're inventorying all the stuff that's in *there.* Don't try to evaluate your degree of mastery of a particular subject. Put down something you've only read a few articles about *(if it interests you)* side by side with a subject you studied for three semesters in school.

Throwaway comes later *(though, obviously, if there's a subject you hate so much you can barely stand to write it down, then . . . don't . . . write . . . it . . . down.),*

When filling this chart out, do not forget to list those things you've learned—no matter how—about Organizations (including volunteer organizations), and what it takes to make them work.

It is not necessary that you should have ever taken a course in management or business. As the late John Crystal used to say, "Who cares how you learned it, whether in school or by sitting on the end of a log?" Examples of things you may know something about (and should list here) are: accounting or bookkeeping; administration; applications; credit collection of overdue bills; customer relations and service; data analysis; distribution; fiscal analysis, controls, reductions; government contracts; group dynamics or work with groups in general; hiring, human resources, or manpower; international business; management; marketing, sales; merchandising; packaging; performance specifications; planning; policy development; problem solving or other types of troubleshooting with operations or management systems; production; public speaking/addressing people; R & D program management; recruiting; show or conference planning, organization, and management; systems analysis; travel or travel planning, especially international travel; etc.

The Subjects Chart

Which column you decide to put a subject in, below, doesn't matter at all. The columns are only a series of pegs, to hang your memories on. Which peg is of no concern. Jot down a subject anywhere you like.

Column 1	Column 2	Column 3	Column 4	Column 5
Studied in High School or College or Graduate School	Learned on the Job	Learned from Conferences, Workshops, Training, Seminars	Learned at Home: Reading, TV, Tape Programs, Study Courses	Learned in My Leisure Time: Volunteer Work, Hobbies, etc.
Examples: Spanish, Typing, Accounting, Computer Literacy, Psychology, Geography	*Examples: Publishing, Computer graphics, How an organization works, How to operate various machines*	*Examples: Welfare rules, Job-hunting, Painting, How to use the Internet*	*Examples: Art Appreciation, History, Speed Reading, A Language*	*Examples: Landscaping, How to sew, Antiques, Camping, Stamps*

Prioritizing
"The Subjects Chart"

When you're done, you may want to let this Chart just sit on your refrigerator door for a few days, while you see if there's anything you want to add.

But when you're sure you've listed all you want to on the chart, it is crucial then to sort and then prioritize all these subjects. See the Prioritizing Grids on pages 15 and 16.

When you've got your ten prioritized Subjects, then go on to the next item, here.

2. Fields Dealing with People's Problems or Needs

The question here is: **if you like to help people, what problems or needs do you like to help them with?** Each of these is a field.

In order to answer this question, it is helpful to fill out either of two kinds of exercises: *A checklist*, or *"fill in the blank."* Better yet, the two together, *like this:*

---

1. Check off any kind of need you think you *might* like to help people with, and then
2. Add *which part of it*, or *what aspect of it*, you find particularly interesting or *appealing*.

The People List

I'd like to help people with their need for:

❑ **Clothing** (people's need to find and choose appropriate and affordable clothing); *and in my case what interests me particularly is_____.*

❑ **Food** (people's need to be fed, to be saved from starvation or poor nutrition); *and in my case what interests me particularly is_____.*

❑ **Housing** and **real estate** (people's need to find appropriate and affordable housing, apartment, office, or land); *and in my case what interests me particularly is_____.*

❑ **Languages** (people's need for literacy, to be able to read, or to learn a new language); *and in my case what interests me particularly is_____.*

❑ **Personal services** or **service occupations** (people's need to have someone do tasks they can't do, or haven't time to do, or don't want to do, for themselves—ranging from child care to helping run a farm); *and in my case what interests me particularly is_____.*

❑ **Family and consumer economics** (people's need to have help with budgeting, taxes, financial planning, money management, etc.); *and in my case what interests me particularly is_____.*

❑ **Retail sales** (people's need for help in buying something); *and in my case what interests me particularly is_____.*

❏ **Automobile sales** (people's need for transportation); *and in my case what interests me particularly is*_____.

❏ **Legal services** (people's need for expert counseling concerning the legal implications of things they are doing, or things that have been done to them); *and in my case what interests me particularly is*_____.

❏ **Child development** (people's need for help with various problems as their children are moving from infancy through childhood, including behavioral disabilities); *and in my case what interests me particularly is*_____.

❏ **Physical fitness** (people's need to get their body in tune through physical or occupational therapy, bodywork, exercise, or diet); *and in my case what interests me particularly is*_____.

❏ **Health services** (people's need to have preventative medicine or help with ailments, allergies, and disease); *and in my case what interests me particularly is*_____.

❏ **Healing** including **alternative medicine** and **holistic health** (people's need to have various injuries, ailments, maladies, or diseases healed); *and in my case what interests me particularly is*_____.

❏ **Medicine** (people's need to have help with diagnosing, treating various diseases, or removing diseased or badly injured parts of their body, etc.); *and in my case what interests me particularly is*_____.

❏ **Mental health** (people's need for help with stress, depression, insomnia, or other forms of emotional or mental disturbance); *and in my case what interests me particularly is*_____.

❏ **Psychology** or **psychiatry** (people's need for help with mental illness); *and in my case what interests me particularly is*_____.

❏ **Personal counseling and guidance** (people's need for help with family relations, with dysfunctions, or with various crises in their life, including a lack of balance in their use of time); *and in my case what interests me particularly is*_____.

❑ **Career counseling, career-change,** or **life/work planning** (people's need for help in choosing a career or planning a holistic life); *and in my case what interests me particularly is*_____.

❑ **Job-hunting, job-placement,** or **vocational rehabilitation** (people's need to have help in finding the work they have chosen, particularly when handicapped, or unemployed, or enrolling for welfare under the new regulations); *and in my case what interests me particularly is*_____.

❑ **Training** or **learning** (people's need to learn more about something, at work or outside of work); *and in my case what interests me particularly is*_____.

❑ **Entertainment** (people's need to be entertained, by laughter, wit, intelligence, or beauty); *and in my case what interests me particularly is*_____.

❑ **Spirituality** or **religion** (people's need to learn as much as they can about God, character, and their own soul, including their values and principles); *and in my case what interests me particularly is*_____.

❑ **I'm interested in working with animals** or **plants** (their need for nurturing, growth, health, and other life cycles that require the kinds of sensitivities often referred to as interpersonal skills); *and in my case what interests me particularly is*_____.

❑ **Other fields** (or people's needs) not listed above, or a new field I just invented (I think): _____.

In each question where it says *". . . and in my case what interests me particularly is . . ."* think whether or not there are *particular age groups* you prefer to work with, *a particular gender* you prefer to work with (*or sexual orientation*), and whether you prefer to work with *individuals or groups, people of a particular background or set of beliefs, or people in a particular place (the armed forces, government, prison, mental institutions, etc.).* If so, write it in.

Prioritizing "The People List"

When you're done, you may want to let this List just sit on your refrigerator door for a few days, while you see if there's anything you want to add.

But when you're sure you've listed all you want to on the List, it is crucial then to sort and then prioritize these Fields. See the Prioritizing Grids on pages 15 and 16.

3. Fields Dealing with Things, Tools, or Products

When you're done with the People list, go on to this third Fields list.

The question here is: **what things or products interest you the most?** (A product may be "a service," incidentally.)

Sampler: do you love to deal with, handle, construct, operate, market, or repair: *airplanes, antiques, bicycles, blueprints, books, bridges, clothing, computers, crops, diagrams, drugs, electricity, electronics, farm machinery, farms, fish, flowers, gardens, groceries, guidebooks, houses, kitchen appliances, lawns, machines, magazines, makeup, manuals, medicines, minerals, money, music, musical instruments, newspapers, office machines, paints, paper, plants, radios, rivers, rooms, sailboats, security systems, sewing machines, skiing equipment, soil, telephones, toiletries, tools, toys, trains, trees, valuable objects, videotapes, wine, wood—or what?*

What things or products do you *love* to deal with? In order to answer this question, you need to compile *a list*. And it is important that it is complete—that is, it's important that it list *all* the things or products that you love to deal with, in any way, shape, or form.

So, the brief *Sampler* above will not do. You need a longer list, and one that identifies what Fields those *things or products* are in. Fortunately, there is such a directory—at your very fingertips. It's called: *the yellow pages*, from your local telephone company. It has it all: things, products, fields, *and*—what you'll need later—the *location* of relevant organizations in your chosen geographical area.

> If you don't plan to stay in your current community for this next job-hunt or career-change, then you will want to write to the phone company in the geographical area you are planning to move to, and secure *its* phone book. In the meantime, you can use the local phone directory for this exercise (just ignore locations).

The instructions for this exercise are simple. Go through the *table of contents* or *the index* of *the yellow pages* (in a phone book you don't mind marking up), and highlight any and every category or field where you think you *might* like to deal with, or handle, or construct, or operate, or market, or repair *that thing, product, or service*. It is best to work your way backward, from Z to A. Then, go back, and looking only at the items you highlighted, circle in *red* the ones that you care the most about. Jot down their names on the next page.

Prioritizing "The Things Phone Book"

When you're done, you may want to let this Phone Book exercise just sit on your refrigerator door for a few days, while you see if there's anything you want to add.

But when you're sure you've listed all you want to on the Phone Book exercise, it is crucial then to sort and then prioritize all these "Things" Fields. Use the Prioritizing Grids on pages 15 and 16.

The Things Phone Book

_____ _____ _____ _____

_____ _____ _____ _____

_____ _____ _____ _____

_____ _____ _____ _____

_____ _____ _____ _____

_____ _____ _____ _____

_____ _____ _____ _____

_____ _____ _____ _____

_____ _____ _____ _____

_____ _____ _____ _____

_____ _____ _____ _____

_____ _____ _____ _____

_____ _____ _____ _____

_____ _____ _____ _____

_____ _____ _____ _____

_____ _____ _____ _____

_____ _____ _____ _____

Putting All Your
Favorite Fields Together

And now that you are done with all three Fields lists, it is time to put all three lists together, and make one unified list of Your Favorite Fields.

And then, choose your top five Favorite Fields, and copy them on the Favorite Interests/Fields of Fascination petal on page 6.

Your Favorite People

With the great emphasis upon the importance of the environment, in recent years, it has become increasingly realized that jobs are environments too. The most important environmental factor always turns out to be people, since every job, except possibly that of a full-fledged hermit, surrounds us with people to one degree or another.

Indeed, many a good job has been ruined by the people one is surrounded by. Many a mundane job has been made delightful by the people one is surrounded by. Therefore, it is important to think out what kinds of people you want to be surrounded by.

Dr. John L. Holland offers the best description of people-environments. He says there are six principal ones:

1. The **Realistic** People-Environment: filled with people who prefer activities involving "the explicit, ordered, or systematic manipulation of objects, tools, machines, and animals." "Realistic," incidentally, refers to Plato's conception of "the real" as that which one can apprehend through the senses.

I summarize this as: R = people who like nature, or athletics, or tools and machinery.

2. The **Investigative** People-Environment: filled with people who prefer activities involving "the observation and symbolic, systematic, creative investigation of physical, biological or cultural phenomena."

I summarize this as: I = people who are very curious, liking to investigate or analyze things.

3. The **Artistic** People-Environment: filled with people who prefer activities involving "ambiguous, free, unsystematized activities and competencies to create art forms or products."

I summarize this as: A = people who are very artistic, imaginative, and innovative.

4. The **Social** People-Environment: filled with people who prefer activities involving "the manipulation of others to inform, train, develop, cure or enlighten."

I summarize this as: S = people who are bent on trying to help, teach, or serve people.

5. The **Enterprising** People-Environment: filled with people who prefer activities involving "the manipulation of others to attain organizational or self-interest goals."

I summarize this as: E = people who like to start up projects or organizations, and/or influence or persuade people.

6. The **Conventional** People-Environment: filled with people who prefer activities involving "the explicit, ordered, systematic manipulation of data, such as keeping records, filing materials, reproducing materials, organizing written and numerical data according to a prescribed plan, operating business and data processing machines." "Conventional," incidentally, refers to the "values" which people in this environment usually hold—representing the broad mainstream of the culture.

I summarize this as: C = people who like detailed work, and like to complete tasks or projects.

According to John's theory and findings everyone has three preferred people-environments, from among these six. The letters for your three preferred people-environments give you what is called your "Holland Code."

There is, incidentally, a relationship between the people you like to be surrounded by *and* your skills *and* your values. See John Holland's book, *Making Vocational Choices* (3rd ed., 1997). You can procure it by writing to Psychological Assessment Resources, Inc., Box 998, Odessa, FL 33556. Phone: 1-800-331-8378. *The book is $29.95 at this writing.* PAR also has John Holland's instrument, called *The Self-Directed Search* (or SDS, for short) for discovering what your Holland Code is. PAR says you can take the test online for a small fee ($9.95) at www.self-directed-search.com.

For those who don't have Internet access (or are in a hurry) I invented (many years ago) a quick and easy way to get an *approximation* of your "Holland Code," as it's called. I call it "The Party Exercise." Here is how the exercise goes (do it!):

On the next page is an aerial view of a room in which a two-day (!) party is taking place. At this party, people with the same or similar interests have (for some reason) all gathered in the same corner of the room.

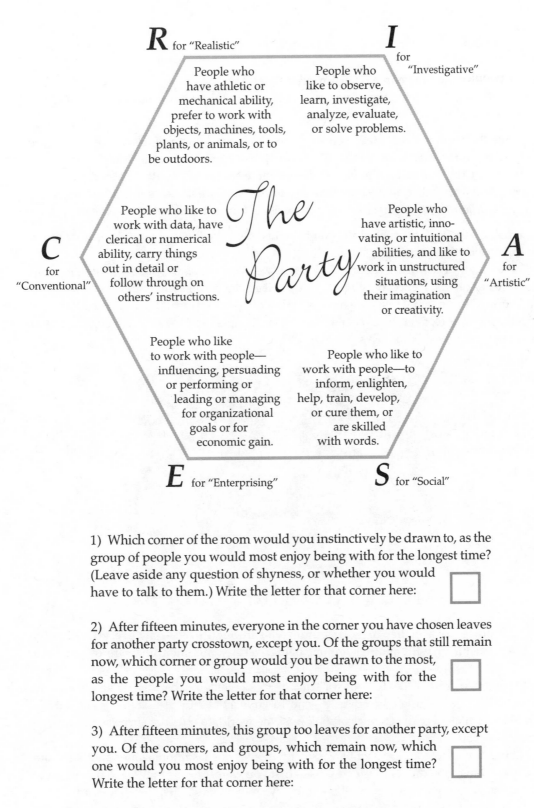

R for "Realistic"

People who have athletic or mechanical ability, prefer to work with objects, machines, tools, plants, or animals, or to be outdoors.

I for "Investigative"

People who like to observe, learn, investigate, analyze, evaluate, or solve problems.

The Party

People who like to work with data, have clerical or numerical ability, carry things out in detail or follow through on others' instructions.

C for "Conventional"

People who have artistic, inno-vating, or intuitional abilities, and like to work in unstructured situations, using their imagination or creativity.

A for "Artistic"

People who like to work with people— influencing, persuading or performing or leading or managing for organizational goals or for economic gain.

E for "Enterprising"

People who like to work with people—to inform, enlighten, help, train, develop, or cure them, or are skilled with words.

S for "Social"

1) Which corner of the room would you instinctively be drawn to, as the group of people you would most enjoy being with for the longest time? (Leave aside any question of shyness, or whether you would have to talk to them.) Write the letter for that corner here:

2) After fifteen minutes, everyone in the corner you have chosen leaves for another party crosstown, except you. Of the groups that still remain now, which corner or group would you be drawn to the most, as the people you would most enjoy being with for the longest time? Write the letter for that corner here:

3) After fifteen minutes, this group too leaves for another party, except you. Of the corners, and groups, which remain now, which one would you most enjoy being with for the longest time? Write the letter for that corner here:

The three letters you just chose, in the three steps, are called your "Holland Code." Here is what you should now do:

1. **Circle them on the People petal, on page 7.**

Put three circles around your favorite corner; two circles around your next favorite; and one circle around your third favorite.

2. **Once the corners are circled, you may wish to write up (for yourself and your eyes only) a temporary statement about your future job or career, using the descriptors above.**

If your "Code" turned out to be IAS, for example, you might write: *"I would like a job or career best if I was surrounded by people who are very curious, and like to investigate or analyze things (I); who are also very innovative (A); and who are bent on trying to help or serve people (S)."*

3. **Finally, here, look over the skills you have just described *in others*, and see how much of this is also true of *you*.**

What I call "The Mirror Theory" holds that we often see *ourselves* best by looking into the faces of others. Hence, once we have described the people we would most like to be surrounded by, in many cases we have also described ourselves. ("Birds of a feather flock together.") So, look over the circled items on your People petal. Are these, perchance, *your* favorite proclivities, skills, tasks, etc.? Or not?

PETAL #4

Your Favorite Values

Values are a matter of what guides you through every day, every task, every encounter with another human being. Yet, we are often unaware of what our values are.

One way to bring values to your consciousness is to imagine that shortly before the end of your life you are invited to dinner—and to your great surprise people have secretly come in from all over the country and all over the world, to attend a surprise testimonial dinner for You.

At the dinner, to your great embarrassment, there is one testimonial after another about the good things you did, or the good person that you were, in your lifetime. No mention of any parts of your life that you don't want to have remembered. Just the good stuff.

So, this brings us to some questions. If you get the life you really want between now and then, what would you hope you would hear at that dinner, as they looked back on your life?

If you do achieve what you want with your life, what about you would you like to have remembered, after you are gone from this earth? Here is a checklist to help you:[2]

It would be a good life, if at its end, people remembered me as one who
(check as many items as are important to you):

- ❏ Served or helped those who were in need.
- ❏ Impressed people with my going the second mile, in meeting their needs.
- ❏ Was always a great listener.
- ❏ Was always good at carrying out orders, or bringing projects to a successful conclusion.
- ❏ Mastered some technique, or field.
- ❏ Did something that everyone said couldn't be done.
- ❏ Did something that no one had ever done before.
- ❏ Excelled and was the best at whatever it is I did.
- ❏ Pioneered or explored some new technology.
- ❏ Fixed something that was broken.
- ❏ Made something work, when everyone else had failed or given up.
- ❏ Improved something, made it better, or perfected it.
- ❏ Combatted some bad idea/philosophy/force/influence/ pervasive trend—and I persevered and/or prevailed.
- ❏ Influenced people and gained a tremendous response from them.

❏ Had an impact, and caused change.

❏ Did work which brought more information/truth into the world.

❏ Did work which brought more beauty into the world, through gardens, or painting, or decorating, or designing, or whatever.

❏ Did work which brought more justice, truth, and ethical behavior into the world.

❏ Brought people closer to God.

❏ Growing in wisdom and compassion was my great goal all my life.

❏ Had a vision of what something could be, and helped that vision to come true.

❏ Developed or built something, where there was nothing.

❏ Began a new business, or did some project from start to finish.

❏ Exploited, shaped, and influenced some situation, market, before others saw the potential.

❏ Put together a great team, which made a huge difference in its field, industry, or community.

❏ Was a good decision-maker.

❏ Was acknowledged by everyone as a leader, and was in charge of whatever it was that I was doing.

❏ Had status in my field, industry, or community.

❏ Was in the spotlight, gained recognition, and was well-known.

❏ Made it into a higher echelon than I was, in terms of reputation, and/or prestige, and/or membership, and/or salary.

❏ Was able to acquire possessions, things, or money.

❏ Other goals which occur to me:_____

_____

_____

When you're done checking off all the values that are important to you, go back, and pick out the ten that you care the most about, and then prioritize them in exact order of importance to you. As always, if you just can't prioritize them by guess and by gosh, then use the Prioritizing Grid on page 15.

The question to ask yourself, there, as you confront each "pair" on the Grid is: "If I could only have this true about me, at the end of my life, but not the other, which would I prefer?" *Try not to pay attention to what others might or might not think of you, if they knew this was your heart's desire. This is just between you and God.*

Put your top six values on the Values petal, in the Flower Diagram on page 7.

Your Favorite Working Conditions

Plants that grow beautifully at sea level often perish if they're taken ten thousand feet up the mountain. Likewise, we do our best work under certain conditions, but not under others. Thus, the question: What are your favorite "working conditions"? actually is a question about "Under what circumstances do you do your most effective work?"

The best way to approach this is by starting with the things you *disliked* about all your previous jobs, using the following chart to list these. The chart, as you can see, has three columns, and you fill them out in the same order, and manner, that you filled out the geography chart earlier. Here too, you may copy this chart onto a larger piece of paper if you wish, before you begin filling it out. *Column A may begin with such factors as: "too noisy," "too much supervision," "no windows in my workplace," "having to be at work by 6 a.m.," etc.*

Of course, when you get to Column B, you must rank these factors that are in Column A, in their exact order of importance, to you.

As always, if you are baffled as to how to prioritize these factors in exact order, use the Prioritizing Grid on page 15 or 16.

The question to ask yourself, there, as you confront each "pair" is: "If I were offered two jobs, and in the first job I would be rid of this first distasteful working condition, but not the second; while in the second job, I would be rid of the second distasteful working condition, but not the first, which distasteful working condition would I choose to get rid of?"

Note that when you later come to Column C, the factors will be already prioritized. Your only job, there, is to think of the "positive" form of that factor that you hated so much (in Column B). (It is not always "the exact opposite." For example, *too much supervision*, listed in Column B, does not always mean *no supervision*, in Column C. It *might* mean: *a moderate amount of supervision, once or twice a day.*)

Once you've finished Column C, enter the top five factors from there on the Working Conditions petal of the Flower Diagram, on page 7.

	Column A — Distasteful Working Conditions	*Column B* — Distasteful Working Conditions Ranked	*Column C* + The Keys to My Effectiveness at Work
Places I Have Worked Thus Far in My Life	*I Have Learned from the Past That My Effectiveness at Work Is Decreased When I Have to Work Under These Conditions:*	*Among the Factors or Qualities Listed in Column A, These Are the Ones I Dislike Absolutely the Most (in order of Decreasing Dislike):*	*The Opposite of These Qualities, in Order:* *I Believe My Effectiveness Would Be at an Absolute Maximum, If I Could Work Under These Conditions:*

Level & Salary

Salary is something you must think out ahead of time, when you're contemplating your ideal job or career. Level goes hand in hand with salary, of course.

1. **The first question here is at what level would you like to work, in your ideal job?**
    Level is a matter of how much responsibility you want in an organization:

    ❑ Boss or CEO (this may mean you'll have to form your own business)

    ❑ Manager or someone under the boss who carries out orders, but also gives them

    ❑ The head of a team

    ❑ A member of a team of equals

    ❑ One who works in tandem with one other partner

    ❑ One who works alone, either as an employee or as a consultant to an organization, or as a one-person business.

    Enter a two- or three-word summary of your answer, on the Salary and Level petal of the Flower Diagram, on page 6.

2. **The second question here is what salary would you like to be aiming at?**
    Here you have to think in terms of minimum or maximum. **Minimum** is what you would need to make, if you were just barely "getting by." And you need to know this *before* you go in for a job interview with anyone *(or before you form your own business, and need to know how much profit you must make, just to survive).*

    Maximum could be any astronomical figure you can think of, but it is more useful here to put down the salary you realistically think you could make, with your present competency and experience, were you working for a real, *but generous*, boss. (If this maximum figure is still depressingly low, then put down the salary you would like to be making five years from now.)

    Make out a detailed outline of your estimated expenses *now*, listing what you need *monthly* in the following categories:[3]

Housing

    Rent or mortgage payments . . . . $ _____

    Electricity/gas . . . . $ _____

    Water . . . . $ _____

    Telephone. . . . . $ _____

    Garbage removal . . . . $ _____

    Cleaning, maintenance, repairs[4] . . . . $ _____

Food

    What you spend at the supermarket

    and/or meat market, etc. . . . . $ _____

    Eating out. . . . . $ _____

Clothing

    Purchase of new or used clothing . . . . $ _____

    Cleaning, dry cleaning, laundry . . . . $ _____

Automobile/transportation[5]

    Car payments . . . . $ _____

    Gas . . . . $ _____

    Repairs . . . . $ _____

    Public transportation (bus, train, plane) . . . . $ _____

Insurance

    Car . . . . $ _____

    Medical or health care. . . . . $ _____

    House and personal possessions. . . . . $ _____

    Life . . . . $ _____

Medical expenses

    Doctor's visits . . . . $ _____

    Prescriptions . . . . $ _____

    Fitness costs . . . . $ _____

Support for other family members

    Child-care costs (if you have children) . . . . $ _____

    Child support (if you're paying that) . . . . $ _____

    Support for your parents (if you're helping out) . . . . $ _____

Charity giving/tithe (to help others) . . . . $ _____

School/learning

    Children's costs (if you have children in school) . . . . $ _____

    Your learning costs (adult education,

    job-hunting classes, etc.) . . . . $ _____

Pet care *(if you have pets)*. . . . . $ _____

Bills and debts *(Usual monthly payments)*

    Credit cards . . . . $ _____

    Local stores. . . . . $ _____

    Other obligations you pay off monthly . . . . $ _____

Taxes

    Federal[6] *(next April's due, divided by*

    months remaining until then) . . . . $ _____

    State *(likewise)* . . . . $ _____

    Local/property *(next amount due, divided by*

    months remaining until then) . . . . $ _____

    Tax-help *(if you ever use an accountant,*

    pay a friend to help you with taxes, etc.) . . . . $ _____

Savings . . . . $ _____

Retirement (Keogh, IRA, SEP, etc.) . . . . $ _____

Amusement/discretionary spending

    Movies, video rentals, etc. . . . . $ _____

    Other kinds of entertainment . . . . $ _____

    Reading, newspapers, magazines, books. . . . . $ _____

    Gifts *(birthday, Christmas, etc.)* . . . . $ _____

    Vacations . . . . $ _____

Total Amount You Need Each Month . . . . $ _____

Multiply the total amount you need each month by 12 to get the yearly figure. Divide the yearly figure by 2,000, and you will be reasonably near the *minimum* hourly wage that you need. Thus, if you need $3,333 per month, multiplied by 12 that's $40,000 a year, and then divided by 2,000, that's $20 an hour.

Parenthetically, you may want to prepare two different versions of the above budget: one with the expenses you'd ideally *like* to make, and the other a minimum budget, which will give you what you are looking for, here: the floor, below which you simply cannot afford to go.

Enter the maximum, and minimum, on your Salary and Level petal on the Flower Diagram on page 6.

Optional Exercise: You may wish to put down other rewards, besides money, that you would hope for, from your next job or career. These might be:

❏ Adventure

❏ Challenge

❏ Respect

❏ Influence

❏ Popularity

❏ Fame

❏ Power

❏ Intellectual stimulation from the other workers there

❏ A chance to exercise leadership

❏ A chance to be creative

❏ A chance to make decisions

❏ A chance to use my expertise

❏ A chance to help others

❏ A chance to bring others closer to God

❏ Other:

If you do check off things on this list, arrange your answers in order of importance to you, and then add them to the Salary and Level petal on page 6.

Done!

Voila! Your Flower Diagram should now be complete. At this point, take a hard look at it, and see how this new knowledge of yourself and your ideal job helps you to narrow down what it is you are looking for.

ENDNOTES

1. For the curious, "animals" are placed in this category with "people," because **the skills** required to deal with animals are more like those used with people, than like those used with "things."

2. I am indebted to Arthur Miller, of People Management, Inc., for many of these ideas.

3. If this kind of financial figuring is not your cup of tea, find a buddy, friend, relative, family member, or *anyone*, who can help you do this. If you don't know anyone who could do this, go to your local church, synagogue, religious center, social club, gym, or wherever you hang out, and ask the leader or manager there, to help you find someone. If there's a bulletin board, put up a notice on the bulletin board.

4. If you have extra household expenses, such as a security system, be sure to include the quarterly (or whatever) expenses here, divided by three.

5. Your checkbook stubs will tell you a lot of this stuff. But you may be vague about your cash or credit card expenditures. For example, you may not know how much you spend at the supermarket, or how much you spend on gas, etc. But there is a simple way to find out. Just carry a little notepad and pen around with you for two weeks or more, and jot down *everything* you pay cash (*or use credit cards*) for—*on the spot, right after you pay it.* At the end of those two weeks, you'll be able to take that notepad and make a realistic guess of what should be put down in these categories that now puzzle you. (*Multiply the two-weeks figure by two, and you'll have the monthly figure.*)

6. Incidentally, for U.S. citizens, looking ahead to next April 15, be sure to check with your local IRS office or a reputable accountant to find out if you can deduct the expenses of your job-hunt on your federal (and state) income tax returns. At this writing, some job-hunters can, if—big IF—this is not your first job that you're looking for, if you haven't been unemployed too long, and if you aren't making a career-change. Do go find out what the latest "ifs" are. If the IRS tells you you are eligible, keep careful receipts of everything related to your job-hunt, as you go along: telephone calls, stationery, printing, postage, travel, etc.

NOTES

Ten Speed Press
Box 7123
Berkeley, California 94707
www.tenspeed.com

Distributed in Australia by Simon and Schuster Australia, in Canada by Ten Speed Press Canada,
in New Zealand by Southern Publishers Group, in South Africa by Real Books,
and in the United Kingdom and Europe by Publishers Group UK.

Cover design by Betsy Stromberg
Text design by Linda Davis, Star Type

Library of Congress Cataloging-in-Publication Data
on file with the publisher

Printed in the United States of America

7 8 9 10 — 10 09 08